MW00415695

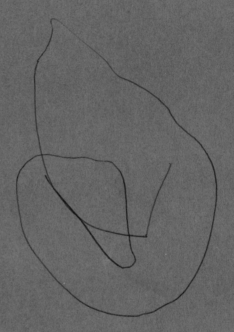

VeggieTales

ADVENTURES OF
THE GOOD GUYS

Little Joe, Lyle the Kindly Viking and LarryBoy!

This book belongs to:

_____

Adapted by Karen Poth
Illustrated by Paul Conrad

Based on the VeggieTales® videos *The Ballad of Little Joe, Lyle the Kindly Viking and LarryBoy* and *The Fib from Outer Space*.

ISBN: 978-1-60587-415-9
Printed in the United States of America.

veggietales.com

Then you will know the truth.
And the truth will set you free.

— *John 8:32*

Junior and Laura needed one more plate for their tea party.

"I know just where to get one," Junior said as he climbed the bookcase. On the top shelf was his father's very special Art Bigotti collector's plate.

WOBBLE, WOBBLE . . . CRASH! The plate fell and broke into a hundred pieces!

"I gotta go," Laura said. She didn't want to be around when Junior's dad got home.

Junior was all alone until suddenly . . . from under the table popped a small purple alien. "The name is Fibrillious Minimus," the alien said. "But you can call me Fib!"

"What you need is a story," Fib told Junior. "Make up a story about how somebody else broke that plate."

"You mean . . . lie?" Junior asked.

"No, no, no. It's just a little fib," Fib said. "A little fib can't hurt anybody."

Before Junior knew it, his father was home. Junior had some explaining to do.

"It's Laura's fault.
She broke the plate.
I tried to stop her.
She said she had to demonstrate the apple chopper.
The apple chopper worked just great.
It chopped right through your bowling plate!
It's Laura's fault. She broke the plate. It's true."

Junior's father believed the story. And as Junior headed out to play with his new friend, Fib, he noticed something very strange—little Fib had gotten bigger!

Out on the street, Junior met Percy Pea. "Junior," Percy said, "Laura got in trouble for breaking that plate. But she says she didn't do it. Who's telling the truth?"

Junior thought for a minute. Then he said,

"It's Lenny's fault.
He broke the plate.
He's very naughty.
Just how was I to know he hated Art Bigotti?
He gave it to a crocodile,
who chewed it up for quite a while.
It's Lenny's fault. He broke the plate.
It's true."

He turned to leave with
Fib, who was now even
taller than Junior!

Later that day, Laura, Lenny, and Percy spotted Junior walking home. "There he is!" Laura shouted. Junior's fibs had gotten them in a lot of trouble. They were mad!

"That's not what I said at all," Junior explained to his angry friends. "YOU didn't break the plate. It was these space aliens. They came down and they grabbed these cows. And they switched brains with the cows. And the cows with the brains of these space aliens broke the plate."

With those words, Fib came around the corner. He was now taller than the tallest building in Bumblyburg. He bent down and grabbed Junior.

"Help! It's got me! I can't get free!"
Junior screamed.

"Don't worry, Junior, a little fib can't
hurt anybody!" laughed Fib as he
carried Junior away.

Fib thundered down the street, crushing everything in his way. Police Chief Scooter barely got out of his car before Fib's giant foot smashed it flat.

"This is a job for LarryBoy!" Scooter cried. LarryBoy was Bumblyburg's favorite superhero.

High above the city, Junior struggled to get out of Fib's clutches.

"Fib, why are you doing this to me?" Junior asked. "I thought you were my friend."

"That's the thing about fibs, Junior. They grow. Now that I'm big, you belong to me!"

Junior was sure Fib was going to eat him. But suddenly: "Not so fast, monster!" LarryBoy came to save the day! "Drop the asparagus," he ordered.

"Why don't you come here and make me, little purple man!" Fib said, laughing. He was headed toward the water tower with Junior still in his clutches!

LarryBoy launched his super-suction ears
. . . but Fib was too fast for the superhero. In
one HUGE sweeping motion, the monster
grabbed LarryBoy tightly with his other hand.

Just as everything was looking completely hopeless, Alfred radioed from the LarryCave. "Master Larry," he said, "the computer says the monster is a lie. The whole thing is a big lie!"

"How can I stop it?" LarryBoy screamed as the monster squeezed him tighter and tighter.

"According to my calculations, YOU can do . . . NOTHING," Alfred said. "Fib can only be stopped by—"

Before Alfred could finish, Fib
stuck LarryBoy in his mouth!

Junior squirmed in the monster's grip. "I did it!" he yelled. "I broke the plate!"

With those words, LarryBoy popped out of the monster's mouth. Fib began to shrink.

"I said Laura and Lenny broke the plate, but it was me," Junior confessed. "It was all a big lie!"

As Junior told the truth, Fib got smaller and smaller, until he was so small that no one was afraid anymore.

"Dad," Junior finally said, "I'm really sorry I broke your plate."

"Oh, Junior," Dad Asparagus said with a smile. "I'm sure it was an accident. Let's just make sure that from now on, we tell the truth the first time!"

We know that in all things
God works for the good of
those who love him.

— Romans 8:28a

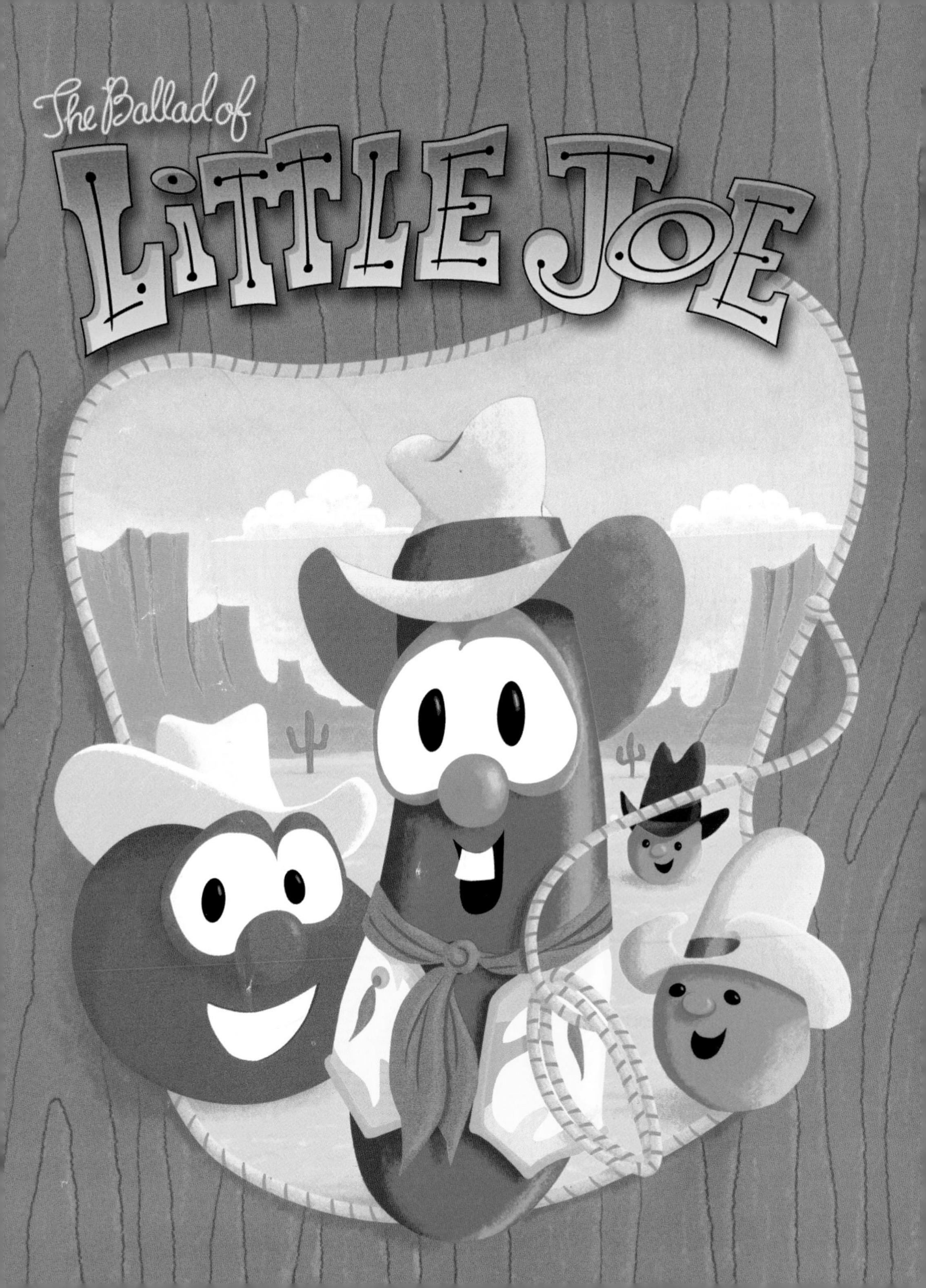
The Ballad of
LITTLE JOE

A long, long time ago, way out West, lived twelve cowboy brothers. Their names were Reuben, Simeon, Levi, Izzy, Zeb, Gad, Ash, Dan, Natty, and Jude. There was also Baby Ben. But he was too little to go outside. Oh, and there was one more—Little Joe.

Now, Little Joe was different from all his brothers. For one thing, he was a lot taller. And he didn't have a French accent.

But more troubling to his brothers was that
Little Joe was their father's favorite son.

On Little Joe's birthday, his father gave him a beautiful Western vest.

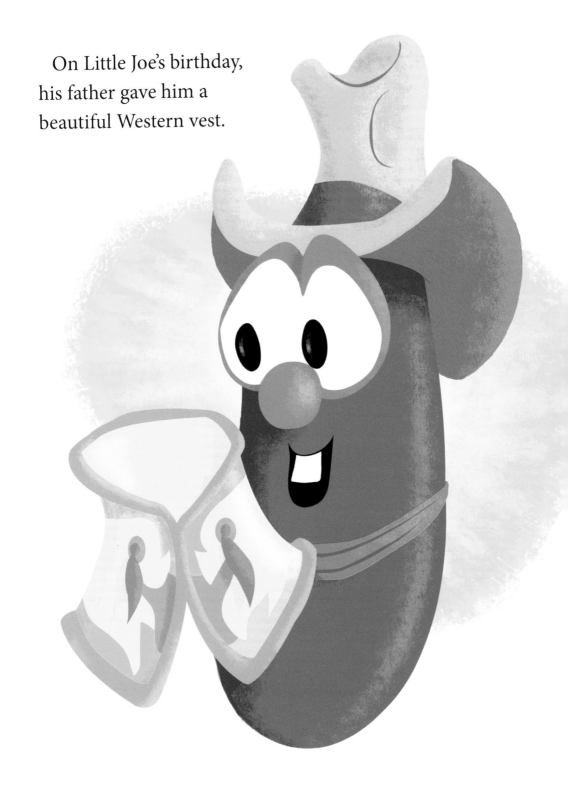

His brothers, who all got mittens for their birthdays, didn't like that one doggone bit. And that was when Little Joe headed into all sorts of trouble!

His brothers were so jealous, they tossed him into an old mine shaft!

HEY, JUDE! Little Joe called out to his big brother from the darkness of the mine. But Jude didn't help. Instead, he sold Little Joe to a band of desperados. That's Western talk for robbers.

Well, those robbers took Little Joe to Dodge Ball City. There they sold him to the owner of the Rootin' Tootin' Pizza Place.

From that day on, Little Joe worked hard selling pizza and root beer.

But that didn't get Little Joe down. He made a bunch
of friends, and after a year, he was named employee of
the month!

EMPLOYEE
of the
MONTH

Unfortunately, that made Miss Kitty, the waitress,
burning mad. Miss Kitty was so jealous that she had Little
Joe thrown in jail.

"Little Joe, why is all this bad stuff happening to you?" asked Sheriff Bob. "Shucks! I don't really know. But God is good," Little Joe answered. "I reckon I just have to keep on doin' what's right."

One day, during an important town meeting, the mayor of Dodge Ball City had a dream. It upset him so much that he asked Little Joe to tell him what it meant. And with God's help, Little Joe did just that.

According to the dream, Dodge Ball City would have seven years of plenty—more food than they could ever eat. Then they would have seven years of severe famine—no pizza and no root beer!

To thank Little Joe for his help, the mayor made him the second most powerful man in Dodge Ball City.

Little Joe got to work right away preparing the town for the hard days to come. During the seven good years, the city stored up plenty of food.

Then, just as Little Joe had said, the bad years of famine came. The people of Dodge Ball City were fine . . . thanks to Little Joe. But Little Joe's family had just one pancake to share. They were doomed!

So all eleven of Little Joe's brothers and his father traveled to Dodge Ball City in search of food.

When Little Joe saw them coming, he wasn't sure he could trust his brothers. So he greeted them wearing a tricky disguise.

But Little Joe's brothers hadn't come to Dodge Ball City to cause trouble. They needed help for themselves and for their father.

"We would like to buy some food from you," Jude told Little Joe.

Little Joe soon realized how God had used all the bad things that had happened to him for good. Thanks to the hardships he had endured, he could now help his family.

Little Joe forgave his brothers, and they had the best family reunion the West had ever seen!

YEE-HA!

Don't forget to do good.
Don't forget to share with others.

— *Hebrews 13:16a*

Once upon a time, in a village by the sea, there lived a band of Vikings.

Just like other Vikings, these "Terrors of the Sea" spent their days pillaging and plundering.

Those are fancy words for taking other people's stuff. The Vikings were stealing. And their boats were so fast that no one could catch them.

But there was one Viking who didn't like to be so mean. His name was Lyle.

Instead of going on the raids, Lyle stayed home
and made crafts—pot holders, to be exact.

After the other Vikings returned from the raids, Lyle would take the small bag of loot they gave him (along with some pot holders) and head out across the sea in his tiny boat.

One day, Sven and Ottar decided to follow Lyle to
see where he was going.

What they saw through their binoculars was troubling, to say the least. Lyle rowed his boat all the way back to the monastery that the Vikings had raided the night before.

But instead of taking more of their things, Lyle
returned the small bag of loot to the monks.

Later that day, Lyle explained to his friends that sharing with the monks was really a lot more fun than stealing from them. "When I share, I get my share of friends," he said. Sven and Ottar liked the sound of that. So they decided not to tell on Lyle.

The next week, Olaf, the biggest, meanest Viking, was out on another raid. "Hey, isn't that Lyle over there?" Olaf asked his crew.

Sven and Ottar tried to distract Olaf so he wouldn't see what Lyle was doing.

"Hey, Olaf! There's a turtle and he's wearing pink pajamas, and he's got a cowboy hat on his lid! Look, Olaf, very close— he's swimming very quickly, chasing down a herd of giant squid!"

"Look, Olaf, Olaf, Olaf!
There's a whale dancing
   with a bear!
Look, Olaf! It's a mermaid!
   It's an ostrich! It's a
   bunny!
Look, Olaf ! Please look
   anywhere but . . . there!"

It was too late. Olaf saw Lyle as he was leaving the monks' island. "That little Viking is in BIG trouble!" Olaf yelled.

The Vikings rowed as fast as they could toward Lyle's tiny boat.

It didn't take long for the Vikings to catch up to Lyle. But suddenly, a huge storm blew in. The waves were so big that all the Vikings were thrown into the sea.

"Hang on, Lyle. Help is on the way!" the monks yelled as they scrambled to save him from the angry waters.

"What about my friends?" Lyle asked when he reached dry land.

"Well, they were mean to us," the monks replied.

"I'm pretty sure God wants us to help everybody, not just those who are nice," Lyle said.

"Oh, right," the monks said. "We're monks. We should know that."

So the monks had a change of heart. They saved all the Vikings from the angry sea that day—because Lyle had made friends with them by sharing.

From that day on, the Vikings stopped their stealing and started being kind. They even started calling themselves the Sharers of the Sea.

Don't let evil overcome you.
Overcome evil by doing good.

— Romans 12:21